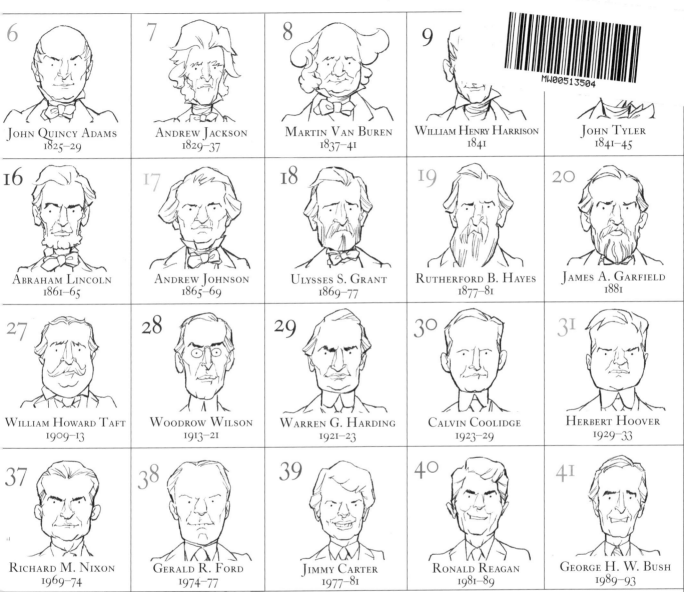

6 JOHN QUINCY ADAMS
1825–29

7 ANDREW JACKSON
1829–37

8 MARTIN VAN BUREN
1837–41

9 WILLIAM HENRY HARRISON
1841

JOHN TYLER
1841–45

16 ABRAHAM LINCOLN
1861–65

17 ANDREW JOHNSON
1865–69

18 ULYSSES S. GRANT
1869–77

19 RUTHERFORD B. HAYES
1877–81

20 JAMES A. GARFIELD
1881

27 WILLIAM HOWARD TAFT
1909–13

28 WOODROW WILSON
1913–21

29 WARREN G. HARDING
1921–23

30 CALVIN COOLIDGE
1923–29

31 HERBERT HOOVER
1929–33

37 RICHARD M. NIXON
1969–74

38 GERALD R. FORD
1974–77

39 JIMMY CARTER
1977–81

40 RONALD REAGAN
1981–89

41 GEORGE H. W. BUSH
1989–93

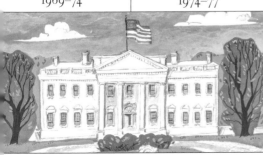

THE WHITE HOUSE HAS BEEN THE HOME
AND OFFICE OF EVERY PRESIDENT OF THE
UNITED STATES SINCE JOHN ADAMS.

The White House
Designed by James Hoban
Built by Many Hands!

Text by **Stewart D. McLaurin** • Illustrated by **John Hutton**

THE WHITE HOUSE *HISTORICAL ASSOCIATION*

Introduction

It takes many people to build a building. Some people lay the stones and other people hammer in the nails. Some people climb ladders and put up the roof and other people hang the windows and the doors. But first, someone needs to create a design that shows where all the walls and doors and windows will go. Today we call people who design buildings "architects." Architects decide whether a building will be tall or short, fancy or plain, big or small.

When George Washington, the first president of the United States of America, needed to have a home built for all the presidents who came after him, he chose a design drawn by James Hoban, an architect who had come from Ireland, a country far away from America across the ocean. Today the house that was designed by James Hoban for George Washington is called "The White House" and it is one of the most famous buildings in the world.

The White House was built by many people, from Scottish stonemasons and Irish builders to enslaved laborers of African descent. Almost everyone knows that the president of the United States lives in the White House, but many people do not know that the house was designed by James Hoban. I hope that more people will come to know more about him and the many diverse builders of the White House so I created this book for you to enjoy. To learn more about the builders, scan the QR code to visit our website all about them.

Stewart D. McLaurin
President, White House Historical Association

The White House is where the president of
the United States lives. It was designed by
a man named James Hoban and built
with the labor of many workers.

James Hoban was born in 1755 in
County Kilkenny, Ireland.

Ireland is an island country across the Atlantic
Ocean from the United States. Many people
living in the United States have family
who came from Ireland.

Growing up, Hoban learned how to make wheels and other useful things. Then he decided to learn how entire buildings are made.

When he was old enough, Hoban moved
to Dublin, the capital city of Ireland.
In Dublin, he went to school and learned
how to design and build buildings.

James Hoban did so well in school that he was
awarded a silver medal. He kept the medal
for all of his life.

Hoban worked on important buildings
throughout the city of Dublin.

When he finished school, Hoban set sail for the United States. It was a new country at that time and in need of many buildings.

When he arrived in the United States, Hoban lived and worked in Charleston, South Carolina. It was here that he became known to President George Washington who was on a trip there.

President Washington needed someone to design the new President's House in the new City of Washington. Hoban came up with an idea and drew out his plans.

Hoban's plan was just what President Washington wanted so he asked him to be the designer and builder of the President's House.

Hoban soon moved to the Federal City that we now call Washington, D.C., to work on the President's House.

Many people from many places labored
to build the house, including Scottish stone
carvers, Irish builders, and enslaved persons
of African descent.

Some enslaved people were sawyers, like Sam Birch and Duvall Lucas. They sawed the large timbers needed to construct the White House.

Other enslaved people made bricks. They formed
them with clay in molds and then baked them in
the many kilns that lined Pennsylvania Avenue.

In 1800 President John Adams and his wife Abigail
moved into the nearly finished President's House,
which we now call the White House. It has been
the home of the president ever since.

Hoban helped create many other buildings in
Washington, D.C., including the Capitol.
He even participated in the Freemason ceremony
with President Washington for the laying
of the cornerstone in 1793.

Not only did Hoban create buildings for the government, but he also helped to found and build the first church in the city, St. Patrick's Roman Catholic Church. He was very active with his church.

In 1814, British troops burned the White House during the War of 1812. President James Madison asked Hoban to help rebuild the White House just as it once was.

After he rebuilt the White House, Hoban's work
continued. President James Monroe asked him
to build the South Portico in 1824.

But he was not done yet. A few years later, James
Hoban built the North Portico on the other side
for President Andrew Jackson. That made the
White House look the way we know it today.

The builders' story is an important part of
the history of the White House. Today, signs near
the White House help us remember those workers
who labored to build the President's House.

About the Author

Stewart D. McLaurin has served as president of the White House Historical Association since 2014. He is also the author of *James Hoban: Designer and Builder of the White House.*

About the Illustrator

John Hutton is a professor of art history at Salem College, and the illustrator of a collection of children's books published by the White House Historical Association. He lives in Winston-Salem, North Carolina.

THE WHITE HOUSE HISTORICAL ASSOCIATION is a nonprofit educational organization, founded in 1961 for the purpose of enhancing the understanding, appreciation, and enjoyment of the Executive Mansion. All proceeds from the sale of the Association's books and products are used to fund the acquisition of historic furnishings and artwork for the permanent White House Collection, assist in the preservation of public rooms, and further its educational mission.

Chief Publishing Officer: Marcia Mallet Anderson; Associate Vice President of Publishing: Lauren McGwin; Senior Editorial and Production Manager: Kristen Hunter Mason; Editorial and Production Manager: Margaret Strolle; Editorial Coordinator: Rebecca Durgin Kerr; Consulting Editor: Ann Hofstra Grogg

Original drawings by John Hutton are dedicated by the artist to Steve McKenna.
Copyright © 2023 by the White House Historical Association

10 9 8 7 6 5 4 3 2 1   Library of Congress Control Number: 2021953106   ISBN 978-1-950273-32-4   Printed in Italy